HOW TO MAKE MONEY WITH REAL ESTATE

EVEN IF YOU DON'T HAVE ANY MONEY

David Bester

FOREWORD

Property investing is one of the most highly regarded subjects of all time, however, due to the complexities and perceived risk many people never take the time to start their property portfolio which itself is a tragedy.

David has taken an overwhelming subject, "dumbed it down" for the average person and provided a comprehensive manual so that absolutely anyone can get started with property investing, even if you don't have a single cent to your name.

Whilst there is no shortage of information about property investing, if you are like most people then you will be looking for straightforward answers to get you from where you are now and into your first property investment without all the hype and bullshit. David delivers exactly that, straight to the point solid information!

In this world, you will find two kinds of people, those who talk and those who do and David is the kind of guy who has been there and done that and continues to do. When he speaks, you can bet your bottom dollar it's based on fact, research, and most importantly expeirnce.

I have had the privilege of doing business with hundreds of people over two decades and I can tell you there are very few people with the analytical skills, the business acumen and ethics that David brings to the table. So my advice, when he speaks pay close attention, there is a lot worth learning.

Justin Harrison

TABLE OF CONTENTS

1. INTRODUCTION

R eal estate investing will probably be one of the biggest investments you take on in your life. It can be a great way to increase your wealth and overall net worth, but in the same breath - it can also be the worst!

Most of us have grown up hearing and believing the following phrases:

- You can never go wrong with real estate
- Don't pay someone else' mortgage, rather buy your own property
- A house will be your best investment

What a bunch of bullshit!

These phrases usually come from the people who have little or no real estate, don't have a clue what their ROI on their property is and 95% of the time don't even know their own net worth. Why would you take advice from these people in the first place?

In this book, I will show you the different types of real estate investments. I will show you the biggest mistakes you need to look out for, the tips that will guarantee that you make a success of real estate investing and I will guide you through the mistakes I made early on in life so you don't make the same.

I will show you how you can invest in real estate if you have absolutely no money at all! Most people think this is impossible, however, I will prove them wrong.

To this day, I own and have owned multiple rental properties and have money invested in different real estate projects globally.

I have personally spent thousands on real estate courses, books, and seminars. They generally had lots of good information but they were drawn out, took extremely long to get to the point and some were very technical.

In this book, I am going to hold nothing back and share every single thing with you in language that even a child can understand.

After you go through this course, you will:

- Have clear knowledge on the different types of property investments
- Know the proper real estate investment terms
- Have the calculations to determine if a property will be profitable or not
- Know how to get into the game even if you don't have money to start with
- Know how to diversify your portfolio to safeguard you against a recession

Let's get started.

2. LOCATION, LOCATION, LOCATION

U nless you live under a rock or have done absolutely no reading when it comes to real estate investing - this is the one phrase you will always come across.

While the location is very important in some cases, I am going to shatter this myth and also tell you why you don't ALWAYS have to buy in the best location.

When should location matter?

When you buy in a good location, the likelihood of your property appreciating in value is pretty good. That being said, when you are looking for investment properties and rental properties then the location will matter a lot.

A good location attracts good clients with money that will most likely pay their rent on time. It also appreciates more in value than it would in a bad location.

When will it not matter?

When you are looking for low-cost real estate and use it to generate rental income. Even though I said that a good location attracts better tenants, a bad location will still make you money.

To illustrate this point I will tell you a story about a guy making millions by having low-cost rental properties in a bad location.

There is a farmer who used his saved money to build lots of low-cost houses (I am talking about 50+) in a bad location which is basically next to a squatter camp. The tenants are minimum wage individuals but this farmer still makes millions from his investment. When a tenant doesn't pay, they simply get evicted and a new one moves in ready with the first month's rent.

Even though it's an industry I personally don't want to be involved in, it still shows you how you can make money from a bad location. Simply put - the volume is there and they all have a need for housing!

The point of this is - conventional wisdom is not always right. Sometimes you need to challenge the rules you were always taught because somewhere in between, there might be huge untapped opportunities.

3. PRIMARY RESIDENCE

E very single person I speak to with the exception of a few successful real estate entrepreneurs believes that a primary residence is a great investment.

While this might be true in some cases, most of the time it's just a damn headache and sucks you dry.

I personally regret buying a primary residence and after renting, I have come to the conclusion that renting is so much easier and more cost-effective.

Here are some of the reasons why I prefer renting instead of buying:

- When something breaks, it's not your problem
- You don't have rates and taxes you need to pay
- You don't have maintenance costs
- Most of the time your money could grow faster somewhere else
- Most of the time you get much more value for money by renting

Look I am not saying that it's a bad idea. What I am saying is you need to make the calculations and see if it really is a good fit for you or not.

Let's take this example:

You see a house you love in a location that you really want to stay in. The mortgage will be $1500 per month but the same house in the same location is available for rent for $1000 per month.

Which one would you choose?

Stripping out all the emotions here (yes that's the real reason you want to buy a primary residence), you would be nuts not to rent it. You can rent the same place for 50% less, you don't have rates and taxes, maintenance, etc.

You can rather use the extra money you are saving to invest in profitable real estate opportunities. Isn't that the reason for investing in the first place...? To find PROFITABLE investments?

Now I can already hear you saying "but I don't want to pay someone else' mortgage". Don't be a dumbass - the numbers don't lie. If the numbers tell you to do it, then, by all means, go ahead. You need to think with logic and not with emotion when it comes to real estate or any other investment out there.

I often hear the same people telling me how they sold a property and made a 30% profit on it. When I ask them if they adjusted this based on inflation, the interest they paid, the maintenance and rates & taxes, I usually just get a blank stare!

Even if they did make a profit, to buy a new home means you have to pay more since the entire property market would have increased during this time.

The moral of the story is - you end up with the same kind of home but probably heavier in debt since human nature tends to upgrade and not downscale.

4. RENTAL PROPERTIES

Rental properties are properties that you rent out to tenants.

The key to being successful in this market is to use other people's money (OPM) which might be a property that is financed by the bank, investors or other sources.

The rental income you get from the tenants should cover your mortgage and all the other extra costs that come along with your property.

The way you get wealthy with this kind of property is to have positive cash flow from the rent that you collect from tenants and in the long term profit off the capital appreciation from the property as well. This investment strategy is a long term game so don't be impatient when you take this on.

Personally I like rental properties, but there are a few things you really need to watch out for when it comes to rental properties.

Losing money in this game is really easy and it can be a real nightmare when you attract the wrong tenants and purchase the wrong property! Not to mention the financial strain it can put on you if your property or properties have a few months without tenants!

I am going to show you the easiest way to determine if your rental property will be a good investment or not! It comes down to 1 simple formula and if you stick to this formula you will not go wrong! The formula simply determines if a property will have a positive or negative cash flow.

Here's the formula:

RENTAL INCOME - MORTGAGE - OTHER EXPENSES = POSITIVE/NEGATIVE

If you follow the formula above and end up on "POSITIVE" then congratulations, your property will most probably be a good investment.

Below are two examples of properties with negative and positive cash flow:

FEES	PROPERTY 1	PROPERTY 2
Rental Income	8000	9000
Mortgage	-5000	-8000
Levies	-1160	-1160
Rates & Taxes	-850	-850
Agency Commission	-800	-800
TOTAL	**190**	**-1810**

As you can see, PROPERTY 1 will be a good investment since it produces positive cash flow from day 1. Each year after that, the rent will escalate as well and so does the earnings you get from the property. After a few years, this will turn into a nice passive income source.

Apart from the rental income, you will be getting, you will also build up equity in the property and if everything goes your way, then your property will also appreciate in value which will increase your net worth.

When it comes to acquiring rental properties, here are a few things you need to be aware of before you purchase one. These tips will save you thousands in the long so don't take these tips lightly. I learned some of them the hard way:

- Make sure the property is cash flow positive from the start.

- Make sure you have enough money to put down for a deposit. Most of the time it will be between 20% and 30%.

- When doing calculations, plan for the worst-case scenario because it rarely works out the way you want.

- Make sure you have enough money saved to cover a few months' expenses should your property be vacant. Believe me - this will happen!

- Make sure you always run a credit check on prospective tenants.

- Use an estate agency to manage your rentals - you don't want to be called up at 11 pm with stupid issues such as a light bulb not working.

- Treat and run your real estate rental company like a real business because it is.

- Make sure you have enough money saved for maintenance - the rule of thumb is 1% of the property value per year.

- If you get a good tenant that treats your place with respect and pay on time - look after them! Don't be greedy and increase their rental with

10% - 15% per year. You can easily get a bad tenant after this and it will cost you a lot more than the increase you would have collected on the rent.

- Don't purchase many properties at once. Make sure you are financially comfortable with your current payments before taking on more.
- Don't just look for deals within your town, look nationally and globally.

These are the most important and basic things to look for when purchasing a rental property. If you follow the tips above, then I have no doubt that you will have a successful rental property business that will provide you with a great source of passive income.

Please see chapter 12 as well where we discuss additional calculations you can use to determine the profitability of a property. They are a bit more technical but they can save you a fortune by directing you to the right decision.

5. FLIPPING HOUSES

The idea of flipping houses is to buy a rundown property at a good price, then fixing it up and selling it again at a profit.

This is typically a short term investment but some people do make it a long term one by moving into the property themselves and over time, fixing it up before selling it.

Depending on your area and profession, flipping houses can be a great way to make money quickly but like any investment, there are also a few risks - especially if you don't know what you are doing.

If you have worked with construction workers before, then you will know that building can be a headache and it never works out the way you planned.

There are always extra costs that come along that you didn't budget for and very few construction workers actually finish a project on time.

That being said, if you are a construction worker

yourself, who can put in the time and get your labour costs down, then this could be a great option for you.

If you decide to go this route, make sure that you get 2 or 3 professionals to look at the prospective property before you purchase it.

This will give you a clear idea of the repair costs involved in the project. Based on this, you can decide to go ahead with the deal or not.

6. COMMERCIAL REAL ESTATE

Commercial real estate is real estate like a shopping mall, shopping centre, office building, or a factory, etc.

With commercial real estate, you can get really good rental income and it's a great way to increase your overall net worth.

Make sure you do your homework when it comes to commercial real estate and make sure you have enough investment capital available because they tend to be quite expensive as you can imagine.

The key to making commercial real estate work is to have an anchor tenant in your building. An anchor tenant is a well-established franchise such as a KFC that guarantees the majority of the rental income each month.

This will greatly reduce your risk in 2 ways:

- Typically don't move often, so you know they are there to stay
- They are well established and usually pay their rent on time

7. REIT

By far one of the easiest ways to invest in real estate is in a Real Estate Investment Trusts (REIT).

A real estate investment trust is a company that owns or operates income-generating properties. It operates much like a mutual fund does with different types of stocks.

With REITS you can start investing with very little capital and I recommend you go this route if you really want to start investing in property and you don't have the massive amount of capital to put down as a deposit for a house.

The nice thing about REITs is that you can decide what industry you want to invest in. You get REITs in commercial real estate, rental real estate, health care, etc.

Your risk is a lot less when it comes to REITs since you don't have the massive amount of capital that you put down as a deposit and you also earn dividends from most of them which are great sources of passive income.

8. CROWDFUNDING & FINTECH

C rowdfunding and Fintech (Financial Technology) has certainly made real estate investing a lot easier, exciting and it gives you a lot more options and diversity when it comes to real estate investing.

With crowdfunding, a group of people invest in a real estate project. The funds typically get put into a trust until the funding is complete and the desired capital is raised. After that, the investors become the owners of the project and the underlying real estate.

The platforms that these crowdfunding models use is called Fintech (Financial Technology). Fintech was designed to challenge the current financial models that we have to deliver better financial services to users across the globe.

With the help of Fintech, you can now make use of crowdfunding to invest in real estate outside of your borders. You have the ability to invest with little capital and you can invest in projects that were historically only available to people with enormous amounts of capital.

There are hundreds of platforms available out there. A simple Google search will deliver lots of results. I recommend you do proper research before deciding on one. The reality is, just like with any industry, you will get some fly by night companies who don't always have your best interests and is just there to make a quick buck.

I suggest you stick to the companies with a proven track record that has been in the industry for a few years and delivered consistent results.

Here are the reasons why I like this model:

- Requires less upfront investment than traditional methods.
- Diversification by investing in different sectors and projects.
- Consistent annual returns.
- Sometimes the returns are higher than traditional real estate investing opportunities.
- Some of the sectors are recession-proof.
- You invest in the physical real estate and not

the share price of a company.

- Less risk since you put up less money and invest with others.

- Gives you the opportunity to invest outside your borders and gives you a hedge against your local currency.

9. TEN LITTLE KNOWN REAL ESTATE INVESTING TIPS

1. Location

We dedicated an entire chapter to location since it plays such a big role when it comes to real estate, however, I think it's really important that I mention it here again. In most cases, location will definitely be very important - even with my example of low-cost housing where you make money based on the volume of units you have.

Even though the location might not attract the best tenant, you still need to be in a location close to public transport or basic amenities. For example, if you build 100 low-cost units 100km from a town with no public transport, then obviously it won't attract many tenants.

2. Schools

Where there are schools, there will be a demand for

real estate. When you invest in real estate make sure you buy within close proximity to schools. Parents don't want to commute for hours to drop off their little ones so it's only logical that they will pay a premium for the comfort of being close to a school. That being said, make sure that it's a school that attracts the kind of tenant you prefer.

3. Building permits

When you start looking for new deals or real estate to acquire, make sure you check the building permits that are being issued. If there are places that are expanding, then it's probably a good idea to buy there.

You will be able to pick up properties at bargain prices since the area isn't established yet and the chances of your property appreciating in value will also be very high depending on the expansion in the area.

4. Jobs

Just like schools, where there are jobs, there will be a demand for housing. People don't want to have long commutes to get to their workplace. It robs them of their time with their families. So make sure when you buy, you look for places where there are jobs in close proximity.

5. Contingencies

Pay close attention to this part because it will save you a fortune and lots of headaches. I'm sure you have heard of someone buying a property only to find out later that it required lots of additional capital due to insufficient due diligence.

When you are making an offer on a property, always make use of contingencies. You don't want to purchase a property only to find out later that it had a cracked foundation? Something like this could ruin your real estate deal completely and result in a massive loss.

Here are examples of contingencies that you can use:

- Purchases contingent to approval
- Purchase contingent to an inspection report
- Purchase contingent to a current home sale
- Purchase contingent to appraisal

6. Buying off-plan

Buying off-plan has a lot of advantages. Properties like this usually sell at a great discount since you are buying directly from the developer and not an agent.

Buying a property off-plan also gives you the option to choose your own finishes and make it custom to your taste which could result in more profit vs a place with cheap finishes. Another benefit is transfer fees - you save a massive amount of money since buying off-plan generally doesn't involve any transfer fees.

Then there is the tax benefit. Lots of countries and states have tax incentives when it comes to buying properties off-plan since they incentivize investors to develop housing in certain areas. I recommend you do your own research or see a tax professional about this.

7. Saving on commissions

If you have a property that you want to sell, then you can make use of Fintech platforms to do this. Thanks to the internet, you can now list your property on a Fintech platform where you don't make use of an estate agent, and as a result, saving up to 10% of the selling price on commission.

Some of these platforms are sites like Zillow and Opendoor where you can list your property for free.Other sites let you create a listing on their platform, they arrange for a professional photographer to take pictures of your property and then feed your listing out to all major property websites. You generally have the option to pay a small commission or a flat fee to the platform if the property sells. Examples like this are Eazi and LeadHome which is based in South Africa where I stay, however, most countries these days have their own local platforms.

8. Tax

Purchasing real estate offers lots of tax incentives. Every state and government is different so make sure you see a tax professional when you start your real estate business. It's best to know of these incentives before you start investing since these incentives generally are only applicable to certain types of real estate.

9. OPM

OPM stands for "Other People's Money". The idea of this is to use other people's money or a mortgage to finance a property that you want to purchase and letting the income that you collect from tenants cover the monthly repayments.

After a few years, when you have enough equity built up in your property, you use the equity to finance the sale of an additional property. Follow this process and after a few years, you will have a massive property portfolio built up.

It's a lot like playing Monopoly really... You borrow money to buy the greenhouses and once you have enough, you sell it to purchase the big red buildings. In the end, the idea is to have an enormous property portfolio. It sounds oversimplified but this is how people make money with property.

10. The value

A few years ago I heard someone saying "you make money when you buy a property, not when you sell it." I remember this saying because I think it's a great way of looking at it. Everything in life has a value. When you purchase a property below its value, you are getting a bargain on your deal and it immediately puts you in profit since you can sell the property for a profit.

On the other side of the coin, if you purchase a property at an overvalued price, then you are basically relying on "hope" that this property will appreciate enough to make you a profit. One last thing I need to mention when it comes to the value is, make sure to do your research and get familiar with house values in the neighbourhood you plan to invest in. If you plan on purchasing a house with the intention of doing major upgrades so you can sell it at double the price then I have news for you - things might not go as you planned.

Why is this? If the rest of the houses around you is worth $100,000 then you won't be able to sell your house for much more than this - it doesn't matter how many upgrades you do. The area and the houses around you determine the value. That's why shoebox size houses with ocean views sell for ridiculous prices.

10. INVESTING WITH NO MONEY

A while ago I had one guy attacking me on social media because he believed that we are selling courses on real estate investing to people who have no money and that we are doing them a great injustice by making these claims.

According to him, if you have little money, you won't get finance so you can't invest in real estate. Period!

For a little while, I entertained him in a debate since at the time we didn't even give any advice when it comes to real estate. This guy simply heard what he wanted to hear, assumed that our first course $MONEYSECRET was about real estate (which it wasn't) and then I decided.... Why the hell am I still doing this...?

Arguing with a narrow-minded muppet-like this is a complete waste of time and it's like arguing about religion or politics. Each person has his own view and it will not be changed. So here it goes - you can make money with real estate without having money! It's called "creative finance". All it takes is to take your thumb out of your arse, educate yourself, use a bit of creativity and put in LOTS of time.

As with any investment out there - you have to sacrifice something. If you don't have the money, then you need to sacrifice your time. Stop following conventional wisdom and use your brain to come up with new creative ideas.

There are people making lots of money with real estate and they aren't putting down a single cent. What they do sacrifice however is they spend LOTS of time hunting down great real estate deals.

Let me make it clear to you, and this may come as a surprise - if you find a really great real estate deal, the numbers add up and you have done solid research with an iron-clad business plan, then you won't have problems finding an investor to fund the deal!

Yes, you will obviously take a small minority when it comes to the profit eventually (the investor might take anything up to 95%) but the investor is the one putting down all the money and taking all the risk.

When you have no money, you have to start somewhere and if you are hungry enough and you have the drive, then you can make this happen.

So let me give you some tips when you decide to go this route.

Find a motivated seller

Do lots of research and get on the phone with potential sellers. The key to finding a great deal is to find a motivated seller. A motivated seller can be someone that has to sell urgently because they are relocating etc.

A motivated seller will hardly ever mention the real reason they want to sell so it's up to you to ask lots of questions until you get to the real reason they are selling. When you do find a motivated seller, do your calculations and find the amount that will make this a great deal for an investor.

Get a signed offer to purchase

If the seller agrees to your price, then get a signed offer to purchase. In your offer to purchase, make sure you protect yourself just in case you can't raise the capital etc. Remember, you have no money at this stage so you need a plan if you can't find the finance. So as an example, a few contingencies to have in your offer to purchase is "Contingent to finance approval" and "contingent to building inspection" etc.

Tip: Make sure you add as many contingencies necessary to protect yourself from not losing money. Your seller can always find another buyer, you, on the other hand, can be in a bit of trouble if you don't have a proper plan.

Find your investor

Now that you have your signed offer to purchase, you have leverage. You can now approach potential investors to fund your deal. When you do approach investors, make sure you sign an NDA (Non-Disclosure Agreement) with them before you reveal any details. Make sure that you are fully transparent with your investor and make sure that you know the proper real estate terms when speaking to investors such as the IRR, cash on cash return, ROI, etc. We'll cover this in chapter 12.

Investors can smell bullshit from a mile away and even if you have a great deal, if they sense that you don't know what you are talking about, they will cut you short right there. Be confident and do your research before you approach them.

How to find an investor

There are lots of ways to find property investors. Probably the best way to go about this is to build up connections by attending as many real estate meetup groups as you can. Build up as many connections as you can - you never know when the time will come where you will be knocking on their door.

This is just one example of how you can invest in real estate without having money. There are lots of ways people negotiate deals without having the money.

I have even heard about people negotiating deals with the actual sellers to fund the property then there is crowdfunding which we have explained already as well. The key is to become creative and look outside of the norm.

Another way is to act as a "Bird Dog" which is basically a person who identifies motivated sellers and good deals to investors. The investors then pay this person a "finders fee".

Lots of people start out this way and eventually build up enough capital to fund their own deals and put down their own deposits. Until then... use the one thing all of us have, which is time!

So to this guy on social media along with everyone else always following conventional wisdom - take your beliefs and continue living a boring life without any creativity.

11. THE PROPER STRUCTURE

B efore you start investing in real estate, make sure you plan ahead and decide on a structure. Most people start out and just purchase real estate in their own personal capacity, however, I urge you to read the next part diligently and not go that route.

Henry Rockefeller famously said, "The secret to success is to own nothing, but control everything". The first time I heard this, I was young and didn't really understand it until I bought the book "Rich Dad Poor Dad" in high school and finally knew what it meant.

The basic principle of this is to have your assets in separate entities to protect your wealth. What this means is, keep your assets (real estate) in a company to protect yourself from greedy people with bad intentions.

When people know you have money, they will come after you.

Here's an example:

You purchase a property and rent it out. Your tenant slips in the bath and breaks his arm. He now approaches the court, sues you because the bath was unsafe, the court rules in his favour and you have to pay out thousands to settle the claim.

Now, if your property is purchased in your personal capacity and you don't have the funds to pay the plaintiff then they can come after your personal assets such as your house, your car, your furniture, etc.

However, if your property is purchased in a company, then no one can touch your personal assets since it's two different entities.

If you think this won't happen then I challenge you to go have a look at the number of ridiculous lawsuits that people have filed and won.

Even if they don't win, settling a claim for a couple of thousands out of court is still cheaper than going through a lengthy lawsuit.

The bottom line is - it's much safer to have your properties in a company, and controlling the company instead. Not only does it protect your wealth but you also get more tax incentives.

When you decide to open a company, choose the type of real investment first and then approach a professional to advise you on the correct structure.

12. IMPORTANT TERMINOLOGY

When it comes to real estate investing, there's quite a bit of terminology that you need to familiarize yourself on. Here are the most common ones that you will come across:

Adjustable-Rate Mortgage

This is a mortgage where the interest rate fluctuates at different intervals based on market conditions.

Appraisal

This is generally done by a lender to determine the value of a property.

Appreciation

The appreciation is the amount that the property has increased over time.

Assessed Value

This is the value of a property that is determined by an assessor.

Bird Dog

These are people who are paid a fee to identify motivated sellers and distressed properties on behalf of others. If you have no money to invest in a property, then this would be a good route to follow.

Buyer's Market

This is a trend when property prices tend to be lower since more people are looking to sell a property.

Cash Flow

The cash flow is money that is left after all expenses on a property is paid. This might be your mortgage, utilities, levies, rent, agency commission, etc. The cash flow can be positive or negative. You should always aim for positive of course.

Cash on Cash Return

The Cash on Cash Return is the annual cash flow before tax, divided by the total cash invested times 100. This gives you the cash on cash return expressed as a percentage.

So let's assume you put a $25,000 down payment on a property. This is your total cash invested. Then let's assume your annual cash flow is $4,000.

$4000 / $25,000*100 = 16%.

Cash Reserves

This is money that is put aside after the down payment and closing costs are paid to allow for emergencies.

Cap Rate

The capitalization rate is the total net operating income, divided by the current market value of a property, times 100.

For example, let's say your annual NOI is $1,000 and your property is worth $100,000. Then $1,000 (NOI) divided by $100,000 (selling price) times 100 = 10%.

Closing

A meeting at which a buyer and seller finalize a real estate transaction.

Comparative Market Analysis

Comparative market analysis is to compare similar properties within the same area to determine its value.

Contingencies

As mentioned before, contingencies are there to protect buyers and sellers. It's conditions that have to be met before the purchase of a property can close. This could be things like finance approval, appraisals, etc.

Debt-to-Income Ratio

This is calculated by taking your monthly debt repayments and dividing it by your gross monthly income, multiplied by 100. This gives you your debt to income ratio percentage.

Here's an example. Let's say you earn $5000 per month. Your current debt is $1,000 and the new monthly repayment on the house you want to buy is $500. Your total debt will then be $1,500. So you take $1,500 (total debt) divided by $5000 (gross income) times 100 equals to 30%

Distressed Property

This is when an owner defaults on his mortgage, doesn't pay property taxes or the property is condemned.

Debt Service Coverage Ratio

Typically, the debt service coverage ratio (DSCR) is used by a bank or a lender to calculate the income vs expenses on an investment property.

Escrow

A financial account that is funded by a homeowner's mortgage payments, used to pay for homeowners' insurance and property taxes.

Exit Strategy

This refers to how an investor will cash out on an investment property. This could include renting the property out or selling a rehabbed property.

Equity

The equity is the difference between the current market value of a property and the amount that an owner owes on a property. So basically as you start paying towards your mortgage, you are slowly building equity in the property.

Fixed-Rate Mortgage

This is a mortgage with a fixed interest rate that you will pay during the term of the mortgage

Flipping

This is where you buy a run-down house and make improvements to it with the idea of selling it for profit.

Hard Money Loan

This is usually loans from private investors or private organizations. They are generally quicker than a bank and have a higher interest as well since the investor/company is taking a risk.

Internal Rate of Return

The internal rate of return is the discount rate at

which the net present value (NPV) of all cash flows from an investment or project is zero. This metric is used to estimate the profitability of potential investments.

Loan-to-value (LTV)

Loan-to-value (LTV) is a ratio utilized by lenders to measure the amount of the loan relative to the value of a property. Lenders often show preference to properties with lower LTVs ratios by offering lower interest rates. Buyers can lower the ratio by making a larger down payment.

Multi-family housing

Multi-family properties is a residential building with multiple residential units within the building.

Motivated Sellers

This is someone that has to sell urgently. You can generally negotiate much better deals with a motivated seller because of their urgent need to make the sale.

Net Operating Income (NOI)

This is calculated annually after all the operating expenses are deducted from an investment property. This might be tax, maintenance fees, management fees, etc. The net operating income doesn't take into account for mortgages. This is the main difference between cash flow and NOI.

Net Present Value (NPV)

The Net Present Value (NPV) is the calculation that you use to get the present value of an investment. You do this by discounting all future cash flows to get the present value and then subtracting it from the initial present investment. If the NPV is greater than 0 then it generally means that it's a good investment.

Off-Market Property

An off-market property is one that has been sold or is in the process of being sold without any public knowledge.

Pre-Approval Letter

A pre-approval letter is usually offered by a bank before you start looking for a home to state the amount that you can apply for and what they typically would approve.

Predictive Analytics

Predictive analytics is the means of using historical data and current data to predict future property trends.

Proof Of Funds

This is basically a declaration from a financial institution where they verify that a buyer has enough funds to proceed with a purchase offer.

Real Estate Owned (REO)

This is a property that is owned by a lender such as a bank.

Refinancing

Homeowners sometimes restructure their mortgage by getting a new one. They usually do this to get a better interest rate. The process is called refinancing.

Rehabilitation

This is the maintenance of a property that has to be done to make it tenant-friendly.

Remote Investing

Remote investing refers to investors who invest in property outside of their geographical areas.

Return On Investment (ROI)

Return on investment (ROI) is where you take the net profit, divided by the initial investment, times 100. The higher the ROI, the higher the returns will be.

An example if your net profit is $2,000 and your down payment (initial investment) was $25,000 then your ROI will be 8%.

Seller's Market

This is a trend when property prices tend to be higher since more people are looking to purchase the property.

Sectional Title

Sectional title refers to separate ownership of units in a complex or development.

Single-Family Rentals (SFRs)

A single-family rental or SFR is a free-standing residential property designed to house one family that was purchased by an investor and rented to a tenant.

Skin In The Game

Skin in the game simply means that you also have money invested in the project and also carry risk in a monetary form.

Turn-Key Property (TKP)

A turn-key property or TKP is a property that has been purchased, rehabbed and rented to a tenant and is now for sale to another investor.

Tenant Screening

This is where you screen potential tenants to find out if they will be a proper fit for your unit. This generally includes credit score screening and background checks.

Vacancy Provision

A vacancy provision is a money that investors put aside for future vacancies. The rule of thumb is to put 6% of the monthly rental for vacancies and 6% for maintenance.

1% Rule

This rule states that the rent collected from an investment property shouldn't be less than 1% of the purchase price of the property. If it is less then it most probably won't be a good investment.

13. CLOSING THOUGHTS

Congratulations on making it to the end. I know I covered a lot of information in 35 pages but as you have probably noticed, the point I was trying to get at was to put out all the important information you need, stripping all the fluff and giving you the actionable points to follow.

What I highly suggest you do now is take chapter 12 and really familiarize yourself with the terminology and calculations. Watch a few YouTube videos until you know how to use these in real life. When you do, take some real-life examples and practice by determining if the property will be a good investment or not. If you do it enough, you will eventually find one and the more you practice, the better you will become at it.

Decide which type of property investment you want to pursue and immerse yourself into learning. There really is almost no subject you can't teach yourself on YouTube these days. The more you learn, the luckier you will become in the real world.

Good luck and I wish you all the best.

ACKNOWLEDGEMENTS

I want to thank my parents, Yvonne & Albert Kilian, for the values they taught me growing up. It shaped me into the adult that I am today, and I want to thank you for always encouraging me in my business and personal life.

I want to thank my wife, Stephanie Bester, for always being there for me and supporting every decision I make. I have indeed found the perfect partner and couldn't ask for better.

I also want to thank my business partners, Chris du Toit, Laura Palmieri, Justin Harrison, and Dale Maxwell, for their support and fantastic business ethics. We make a great team.

Then finally, I want to thank my first mentor, business partner, and friend, Justin Harrison. The advice you have given me over the years is priceless, and it's a great honour to serve with you on this journey in Global Money Academy.

First printing, 2019.

Team 6 Investment Holdings Ltd.
5th Floor, Ritter House,
Wickhams Clay II,
Road Town, Tortola
British Virgin Islands

www.globalmoneyacademy.com

Made in the USA
Middletown, DE
24 July 2023

35622600R00035